Excerpts and illustrations by Tove Jansson © Moomin Characters Ltd., Finland
Text © Sami Malila and WSOY
Original title: "Nipsun mietekirja"
First published in Finnish by Werner Söderström Corporation (WSOY) in 2009,
Helsinki, Finland
Translation into English © Oliver Wastie
First published in English by SelfMadeHero in 2011
A division of Metro Media Ltd
5 Upper Wimpole Street London W1G 6BP
www.selfmadehero.com

Publishing Director: Emma Hayley
Marketing Director: Doug Wallace
Editorial Assistant: Lizzie Kaye
Cover Designer: Kurt Young
With thanks to: Nick de Somogyi

This work has been published with the financial assistance of
FILI – Finnish Literature Exchange

FINNISH LITERATURE EXCHANGE

A CIP record for this book is available from the British Library

978-1-906838-23-2

10 9 8 7 6 5 4 3 2 1

Printed and bound in China

To the Reader

THE BELOVED MOOMIN STORIES OF TOVE JANSSON ARE
FULL OF THRILLING ADVENTURES, EXUBERANT HUMOUR,
ETERNAL TRUTHS AND TIMELESS WISDOM.

IN THIS BOOK OF THOUGHTS WE MEET SNIFF. WE ALSO
MEET HIS PARENTS, THE MUDDLER AND THE FUZZY.
SNIFF IS A SWEET-NATURED LITTLE CREATURE WHO
OFTEN HAS TO OVERCOME HIS NERVES TO JOIN HIS
FRIEND MOOMINTROLL IN ALL MANNER OF ADVENTURES,
SHOWING THAT A LITTLE COURAGE IS ALL THAT IS
NEEDED TO LIVE AN EXCITING LIFE.

WE HOPE YOU ENJOY THE WISE WORDS AND ENCHANTING
INSIGHTS OF SNIFF'S BOOK OF THOUGHTS!

Excerpts and illustrations are from the following WSOY editions of the Moomin books, translated from the original Swedish into Finnish:

MUUMIT JA SUURI TUHOTULVA

MUUMIPEIKKO JA PYRSTÖTÄHTI

TAIKURIN HATTU

NÄKYMÄTÖN LAPSI JA MUITA KERTOMUKSIA

MUUMIPAPAN UROTYÖT

VAARALLINEN MATKA

"Happy?" Sniff's furrowed snout smoothed out.

He looked at Moominpappa and shouted suddenly with happiness: "Of course! Did she also have a button collection?"

"Several," said Moominpappa with relief.

"Hurray!" shrieked Sniff.

IT was a totally fantastic night!

Never before had any veranda been witness to so many questions, cries of joy, embraces and answers. The Muddler and the Fuzzy spread out their button collections on the rug and there and then bestowed them on their son.

"LET'S wrap ourselves up in the blankets and wait until the sun comes up."

So they sat in a row on the shore, huddled up against each other. Sniff wanted to sit in the middle because he felt that was the safest place to be.

"PAPPA, wasn't it then that you ran away with the Hattifatteners?" asked Moomintroll.

"Well now," Moominpappa said, blushing, "I might have. But that happened much, much later on. I thought that I would leave it out of this book altogether."

"I think you really have to write about it," said Sniff. "Is that when you lived a wicked life?"

"CAN you dive with your eyes open?" asked Moomintroll.

"I can, but I don't want to," replied Sniff. "You never know what you might see down there!"

"You're too small to know everything," retorted Moomintroll.

"Who, me?" shouted Sniff. "Do you think it's right to ask me along on this expedition and not even tell me what we are supposed to be looking for?"

"Goodness me," said Sniff. And a fierce inner battle ensued, for he always longed for nice things.

Standing Up for Good Manners!

"PLEASE CAN I HAVE ONE?" SQUEAKED SNIFF.

MOOMINTROLL looked at the Snork Maiden in surprise, but then it crossed his mind that maybe this was a new game. He let out an affectionate laugh and cried happily: "I am the King of California!"

"And I am the Snork's sister," said the Snork Maiden. "This is my brother."

"My name is Sniff," said Sniff.

"YOU swore!" shouted Sniff, aghast.

"PAPPA is reading his memoirs aloud," explained Moomintroll.

"Is it fun?" asked Moominmamma.

"Terribly," replied Moomintroll.

"That's wonderful," said Moominmamma. "Just don't read anything to the children that puts us in a bad light, dear. Say something like 'blah, blah, blah' instead. Would you like a cigar?"

"Don't let him smoke!" shouted Sniff. "The Hemulen Aunt says that it makes your paws shake, turns your snout yellow and makes your tail go bald!"

"ARE we supposed to start arguing now?" asked the Muddler. "Arguing makes me feel sick! I'm so sorry! It's terrible!"

"WHAT on earth has come over the Muskrat?" exclaimed Moominmamma. "He's always so tranquil and dignified!"

"I'm sure that falling out of the hammock must have thrown him off balance," pondered Moominpappa, shaking his head.

"I think he was angry about the fact that we forgot to take him some food," said Sniff.

"WATCH out," said the Hemulen angrily. "You bit my thumb!"

"Oh, I'm sorry," said Sniff. "I thought it was my own!"

THE cellar door opened with a creak and Sniff appeared on the top step with a lantern in one paw and a saucer of milk in the other.

"Hello! Where are you?" said Sniff.

Thingumy and Bob crept further into their hiding place and kept a tight hold of each other.

"Do you want some milk?" said Sniff in a slightly louder voice.

"LET me help!" shouted Sniff...

SNIFF looked at them and concluded that they were a lot smaller than he was. Consequently, he felt more friendly and said in a condescending tone: "Hello! Nice to see you!"

"NOW bow and thank the Hattifatteners for the journey," said Moominmamma. Moomintroll took a deep bow, and Sniff swished his tail in gratitude.

"THERE'S something very strange about paths and rivers," thought Sniff. "When you gaze at their course, your soul becomes restless and wistful. You get a tremendous desire to be somewhere else, to go and see where they end up..."

WHEN Sniff returned home, Moomintroll was just putting up a swing.

"A new path!" cried Sniff.

"All right, let's go there at once. Did it seem dangerous?"

"Very dangerous!" Sniff said proudly. "And I found it all by myself."

"We should take some provisions with us," said Moomintroll. "It might be a very long path – you never know."

Sniff stood in the corner with his snout in his paws and counted aloud. When he got to ten, he turned round and started looking; first in the usual and then in the unusual hiding places.

"The seaside is so ordinary," whined Sniff. "Can't we go somewhere else?"

"Hush, children," said Moominpappa sternly. "Moominmamma wants to swim. Now let's get going."

"Not a single adventure all day," said Sniff, who had been allowed to steer for a while as the current had slowed. "Only the same old grey riverbanks and not a single adventure."

"I think it's very exciting to glide down a winding river," said Moomintroll. "You never know what you'll find around the next bend. Do you know what you're up to? You're chasing after an adventure – and then when it happens, you'll be terrified and run away."

"I'm not a lion," Sniff said, offended. "I like small adventures. They're just big enough."

"Stop eating your dinner at once, children – we'll take the food with us."

"Can I eat what's already in my mouth?" asked Sniff.

"Don't be silly," said Moominmamma.

MOOMINPAPPA tapped the barometer and frowned. "There's a storm on the way!" he said.

"A really big storm?" asked Sniff in terror.

"Look for yourself," replied Moominpappa. "The barometer is showing '00', and that's unheard of. Unless, of course, it's playing a trick on us."

"BUT if a storm does come, we can't go home at all!" said the Snork sensibly.

"That would be great!" cried Sniff. "Let's stay here forever."

"I was transformed because I hid in this hat," explained Moomintroll. "That is the conclusion we have reached. And now we are going to test this by seeing if the ant-lion turns into something else."

"But he could turn into anything!" squeaked Sniff. "He could turn into something much more dangerous than an ant-lion, and eat us all!"

SNIFF rushed under the table and hid himself there.

"WHERE'S Sniff?" asked Moomintroll anxiously.

"Here," squeaked a small voice in the dark, "if this really is me, and not some other piece of rubbish that has been carried here by the wind..."

"I saw it first!" shouted Sniff. "I should be allowed to give it a name. Wouldn't it be fun if its name was SNIFF! It's so short and sweet."

"Hello," shouted Moomintroll. "We've been around the whole island! And on the side facing the open sea there are these terrifically amazing cliffs with a steep drop into the sea."

"And we've seen hordes of Hattifatteners!" said Sniff. "At least a hundred of them!"

Sniff had never in his life been this much afraid – or felt so brave.

SNIFF saw Moomintroll in the distance, standing in the water, dragging and pulling something. Something large! "Pity I didn't find it first!" thought Sniff.

Moomintroll had now managed to rescue his flotsam and was rolling it forward along the sand. Sniff strained his neck – and finally saw what it was. A buoy! A large, impressive buoy!

"Over here!" Moomintroll shouted. "What do you think of this?"

"It's pretty good," said Sniff critically, tilting his head. "But what do you think about these?" And he placed his discoveries in a row on the sand.

"The cork life-belt is good," complimented Moomintroll. "But what will you do with that broken bailing-bucket?"

"It will be fine, you just need to bail quickly," said Sniff.

"IT'S a figurehead!" said Moominpappa, who had sailed the seven seas in his youth. "Sailors used to decorate their ships with a beautiful wooden queen."

"What for?" asked Sniff.

"Say that again!" said Sniff, listening intently. "Rubies! How does he find them?"

"The Hobgoblin can transform himself into anything," Snufkin explained. "And then he can crawl into the ground and even down to the seabed, where treasure is hidden."

"What does he do with so many jewels?" asked Sniff jealously.

"Nothing. He just collects them," said Snufkin. "Just in the same way as the Hemulen collects plants."

"And I'm allowed to pick up and keep everything that drops on the ground," said Sniff.

"I bet he's happy, that Hobgoblin," sighed Sniff.

"Not at all," Snufkin replied. "Not until he's found the King's Ruby."

"Do you think that we might gradually start making our way home?" said Sniff.

"There's magic at work again," said Snufkin. "It's beginning to get tedious."

In the meantime, Sniff ran round the overgrown veranda. "The cellar door!" he shouted in delight. "It's open!"

"We're in luck," said Moomintroll. "The door is open. That goes to show that sometimes it's good to be careless!"

"It was me who forgot to close it," said Sniff, "so I deserve to get the praise!"

"You can carry the provisions," said Sniff. "I can't do it as I have to be the guide."

The silk monkey bounded from tree to tree ahead of them, and she hadn't had so much fun in an entire week.

"Actually it's a bit pointless to run after that small, puny monkey," said Sniff, who was starting to tire. "Let's pretend not to pay her any attention."

"Now we have to take this seriously," said Sniff, who suddenly remembered he was meant to be the guide. "I'll check for side paths, and you knock three times if you see something dangerous."

"What should I knock on?" asked Moomintroll.

"Anything," said Sniff, "just don't speak. By the way, where did you put the provisions? I guess you've lost them. Do I always have to think of everything?"

"And as usual, I have to do the most difficult job," said Sniff gloomily.

"ARE you afraid?" asked the silk monkey.

"Am I afraid? Who, me? Never!" said Sniff.

SHAKING with trepidation, Sniff looked into the cave. It was large, exactly how a cave should be. The rock walls rose evenly and majestically towards the blue sky coming through an opening at the top, and the sand on the floor was just as smooth and white as on the seabed. He dug his paws into the sand and sighed. "I'm going to live here for my entire life," he thought.

"It's a real cave that I found. All on my own!"

"Exactly what I was thinking," Sniff said. "That's what I thought the whole time."

The rain pattered quietly on the roof. It rustled through the leaves and whistled through the forest, and far away it was dripping into Sniff's cave.

"LET'S take lots of food so that there is enough for the silk monkey too!" shouted Sniff. "And lemonade!"

"SOMEONE has been here! In my cave!" shouted Sniff. "How outrageous, how inconsiderate!"

"I guess you aren't – I mean, you don't write poems, do you?" asked Sniff timidly.

"I'll tell you your fortune," said Sniff. "I will place the cards in the shape of a star to see what your future holds."

"It's not the same thing at all only to look at things as it is to touch them and know that they belong to you."

"WOULDN'T it be best to get to land?" shouted Sniff above the roar of the river.

"WHY is it dark?" shouted Sniff.

"REMEMBER that whatever happens will be your fault!" said Sniff, who was bringing up the rear.

"WHAT an incredibly large bird," said Sniff. "I suppose he's lonely high up there all by himself."

SNIFF was standing and counting on his fingers. "Crocodiles, a giant lizard, a waterfall, an underground tunnel, and a condor... Five terrible things to have happen to someone as small as myself!"

FINALLY, Sniff returned dejectedly to the camp. "There can't be a single drop of water left in the whole world," he said. "What would the fish say about that?"

IT was a fun, meandering path. It wound on and on, and would suddenly change direction, and sometimes even doubled back on itself just for fun.

You never tire of walking along a path like that, and probably end up where you want to be quicker than by walking along a straight and boring one.

"I am very interested in comets and I have heard how expert you are, sir, at finding them," said Sniff.

The Professor pushed his glasses on to his forehead. "Have you really?" he said, quite flattered. "Well, then you must be allowed to have a look."

He then adjusted the telescope for Sniff.

At first Sniff was frightened. The sky was completely black and the bright stars glimmered as though they were alive. And far away in their midst something red shone like an evil eye.

"Is that a comet?" whispered Sniff.

"Yes," replied the Professor.

"But it's not moving at all," said Sniff in surprise. "And it doesn't have a tail."